Big Windows

Big Windows

Lauren Moseley

Carnegie Mellon University Press
Pittsburgh 2018

Acknowledgments

I would like to thank the editors of the following publications, in which these poems first appeared, sometimes in slightly different versions:

Arts & Letters: "The Artist As a Disembodied Head, Bleeding on Snow"; *Best New Poets 2009*: "Summer"; *BOAAT*: "Real"; *Copper Nickel*: "Marriage" (as "New Marriage"); *FIELD*: "Cyclops"; *Four Chambers*: "Easter"; *The Greensboro Review*: "When Fog, When Mountain"; *Houseguest*: "Kill Devil Hills" and "Against Me, with Me, Round About"; *Iron Horse Literary Review*: "Marrow"; *The Journal*: "Figment"; *Meridian*: "Mary"; *Mississippi Review*: "A Fine Essence Descending"; *Narrative*: "Biopsy," "Self-Portrait As a Beast with Two Backs," "*Disobedience / is the first right of being alive*," "Onions," and "The Woods Within"; *Pleiades*: "A Warning"; *Sonora Review*: "Illiterate Dream" and "Thanks Be to Big Windows"; *The Southeast Review*: "El Río Manu"; *Southern Indiana Review*: "An Ending"; *Sycamore Review*: "Tail"; *West Branch Wired*: "Something Like Belief" and "The Sound I'll Make"

Many thanks to my teachers at the University of North Carolina at Greensboro and the University of North Carolina at Chapel Hill, especially Stuart Dischell and Alan Shapiro, as well as David Roderick, Linda Gregg, Jennifer Grotz, Michael McFee, and Jim Seay. I would also like to thank the following friends, fellow writers, and talented editors who have offered invaluable feedback and encouragement on individual poems or the book as a whole: Christine Tobin, Josh Watson, Susan Kirby-Smith, Elaine Briney, Sarah Rose Nordgren, Stephanie Rogers, Michael C. Peterson, Kerri French, Erica Ehrenberg, Emily Benton, Shawn Wen, Amanda Shapiro, Lauren Spohrer, Terry Kennedy, and Kathy Pories, with special thanks and love to Joellen Craft, whose care, intellect, and generous spirit have touched nearly every poem herein. I am also grateful to Stephanie Wrenn, Charlotte Bryant, Rebecca Scott, and Gali Beeri for lifelong friendship. Deep gratitude to my friends and colleagues at Algonquin Books and Workman Publishing as well.

This book would not have been possible without the support of the Virginia Center for the Creative Arts, Yaddo, and the Money for Women/Barbara Deming Memorial Fund. Many thanks to *Narrative* magazine and the Writers@Work Fellowship Competition for recognition and support. I would also like to thank Gerald Costanzo, Connie Amoroso, Cynthia Lamb, and everyone at Carnegie Mellon University Press for believing in this book and for their work in the service of poetry.

Most of all I thank my family—my mother and father, Lynn and Phil Moseley, and my sister, Dana Moseley, for believing in me and for showing me the natural world and unconditional love. Deepest thanks to my husband, the poet Ryland Bowman, my brilliant friend, best reader, and great love.

Book design by Danielle Lehmann

Library of Congress Control Number 2017950602
ISBN 978-0-88748-632-6

10 9 8 7 6 5 4 3 2

for my family

Contents

Three

These are modern times, I told myself.
But we are not trapped in them.
—Patti Smith

One

Romance

I am drawn to the window as if it were a fire.

The house rattles a quarter hour, then clouds

cool their engines and streets steam

in abrupt sunlight. Hailstones cover the grass

like clover. I breathe a haze on the glass.

When I step outside to collect the frozen

globes in my hands, they melt too quickly.

Heat and ice. Earth and sky. Stop saying why

I can't have both. I saw them together.

I almost had them.

Figment

White horse   face full of flies
        barn swallows flashing purple
in the field that is more figment   than piece of earth
        gone to meadow   the blooming yellow weeds
            I picked and took

Years ago I had a vision
        a pack of hounds
whipped and driven   by a bearded man
        ran towards me through a field less flowered
            a field of gravel   claws scraping

coming fast   coming for me
        and in the last stretch
they turned   no snarl no growl no pack
        it was only one mutt on a leash and sweet
            walking with its owner through the fog

The need for fear as distant as the pack of hounds
        yet with every gift
of a field like this   at the edges of the forest
        I look for them

Summer

You told me two things while we walked through the gardens:
if you could be any animal, you would be a bear,
and my hair was the color of a wilting magnolia bloom.

It was the last day of good weather. At sunset, empty bottles
of beer and wine glinted everywhere. I banged a tambourine
till my fingers bled. You played guitar and we didn't argue.

I noticed cuts from the jingles in the morning, staring at my hands
while you cursed and threw pots and lids because you broke
a yolk in the pan. It rained all day—bullets of hail in the evening.

We bought tomatoes of every odd color that afternoon:
orange, yellow, green, purple. I was afraid to say I wanted red,
so we got the ones you chose and ate their mealy flesh.

Your moods made me want to shake you like an apple tree
and watch every memory we made fall to the earth. We didn't even
make it to autumn. Cicadas still buzzed fiercely for their mates.

Cyclops

God said I am a cyclops
        in a full-moon voice

One day you will forget
        the way geese crease water

Every life is a renaming
        We were sailing as if we had

another hour to kill
        another hour to live

My name separate
        as a severed hand

I'll always go too far
        for a friendly face

a cup of coffee
        with a moon of milk

One lens of her glasses fogged
        above the mug and she

looked up one-eyed
        straight through me

Deep

I thought I heard him calling *Lauren* but it was a stranger
shouting *Morning*   if the noise of my streets and screens
quieted   I could focus inward   I could find the trouble

but would I even want to?   my inner self wears a hungry face
stretches her long arms towards me   down and down
to the nonsense space   where a tool a bone a clue

lies almost within reach   dig far enough and I might uncover
a primordial answer   the way deep sea divers glimpse
prehistoric fish   I want to find the common ancestor

or at least a grandmother   like Lucy   that early hominin
her bones a constellation   that walked upright   they found her
in a dried-up lake   buried in the bed   no clear cause of death

in bed I drift   not asleep or awake   this journey could last ages
like a quest to find the edge of Earth   we humans cry that life
is short   but I know there's time for it all to go wrong

in ten years a man I loved and finally left   who called my name
like water falling   who didn't love me   could sit beside me
on the subway   take my wedding-ringed hand   and what

would I do?   what wouldn't I do?   even Lucy
with her palm-sized brain   would be smart enough to near
a precipice and walk away   twice in one lifetime

Before Prayer

I walk through an Arctic room of the underworld.

I do not look back because no lover trails me.

Cold is in the cavern ground. Cobwebs

older than my thinning hair clot every corner.

Once, God was the thread connecting all things:

nebulae, antelope, earthquakes, workers.

Then the string snapped. A child

wailed, my debt grew, a film settled

over my eyes. An ordinary day.

No one else casts a shadow in the cave.

The torches burn and are consumed.

It is real, this hollow inside me.

I kneel.

Biopsy

The bear came from behind me, quiet like smoke,
then swiped at my flesh. I dropped to the ground
and did as I'd read: curled on my side, knees to chest,
face buried. The bear's breath was on my neck
and I knew the bite would follow. It was like that,
waiting for the doctor's call.

Iris

One might be enough but I plant another

    bulb to burst open like an urchin

        spiny with leaves that will stretch

    to reach the other flower

because irises want to grow together

Here on the slope with my hands in the dirt

    I hear trembling motors

        lawn mowers and music

    I accept the drone until it's part of me

the silence after: a second life

The Artist As a Disembodied Head, Bleeding on Snow

—after Anselm Kiefer's Winterlandschaft, *1970*

Follow the fuchsia trail from the field to the trees, look up,
and you will find me. My head is not in the dark clouds;
the clouds are in my dark hair, and it is wet.

You will see I am in ecstasy. It is my pleasure to bleed,
to nourish the white space below with color.
But it isn't real. If the blood were real,

it would not be so pink. Some may interpret
the down-turned corners of my mouth to mean
I writhe in pain. I am in pain, but thank God for that.

Without the flowering at my throat and on the field,
you would not be here, looking at me.
I know that, and my eyes are closed.

Self-Portrait As a Beast with Two Backs

I am of two minds, two mouths,
        two tongues licking sixty-four teeth.
Four hands running up and down my oblong body,
        four ears that hear four lungs heaving.

Like a stone at the edge of the ocean,
        I roll in the sand and cannot swim.
A key in a lock, I am closed, a continuous loop,
        as each half that makes me whole

fills, empties, and gluts again.
        Exhausted, androgynous, delirious,
I delight in my many parts, so much
        that the celestial council furrows its brow.

They want to send me the way of the giants
        for my lack of *sacrifice*, a word I do not know.
They threaten to cut me in two, as one
        might divide an egg with a hair.

I want nothing of that, because I want nothing,
        have never wanted, never looked
for another being, never been
        more than four legs, two livers,

four kidneys, two chest cavities,
        two spines and four eyes glassing—
as real and imaginary
        as the worn path of a satellite.

Tail

Hills rolling   trying to say what time it is

       the field a phantom landform   the ridge

a blonde propped up   autumn mountains rising

       from the bare plain   lightning

scratches the far trees   I dreamed

       I had a tail like a bobcat   skinned

stalked the rooms of a house   looking for a place

       to inspect myself   my tail

it was sexual   the rooms too small   always up

       another set of stairs   I felt worry

like a pressure following   I was buried

       from the inside   full of bones

          not mine

Kill Devil Hills

—Outer Banks, North Carolina Coast

They're all of them wasted:
two in the outdoor shower,

two toeing ambergris at the inlet.
Worth millions, they say.

Folks care so much about money.
The sex I can understand.

I peered through a hole in the wood wall
and saw them. Vivid as a fantasy.

I was that boy once, couldn't believe my luck.
I was that girl once, terrified he'd go too far,

unable to stop. No matter who I was,
I didn't know my power.

The Ash Field

You know how in dreams you are everyone:
awake too you are everyone:
I am listening   breathing your ashy breath
—Jean Valentine

I was a giant
carrying a horse on my back
through the ash field

My gait hunched and plodding
I carried the world for once
instead of being carried

There were no birds or the birds made no sound
The horse made no sound
                          Sun behind clouds
Endless horizon

I kept my head down and walked because
the horse would heal

I did not have to shoot

                    I carried it

A Fine Essence Descending

Like sifted flour
A gentle rain
Or blessedness
Perhaps some can feel it
But I feel nothing but years passing
Climbing the stairs to my office
I slip and teeter backwards
In that moment
I am in this world but not of it
No scenes flashing
Instead I'm suspended
Above time and memory
The present bent into two
Possibilities
The sensation through my body
A hum repeating
You have no future
You have nothing
The body nothing
Far above
My whole life at once
Spread out like a quilt
A patch of farmland
Seen from a plane
You could pick it up
Like a handkerchief
My parents my sister my husband
Poems written and unwritten
The children I have yet to bear
Crumpled in the palm of a hand
I hover in air
I am the hand
My hand grabs the rail
Dust swirls and falls
In fluorescent light
My face glazed with sweat
As I climb the last steps

Disobedience / is the first right of being alive
—Paisley Rekdal

A line of ash trees, soldierly,
blighted and falling

in the field behind the lake,
never saying, *No I will not go.*

The brain of the bloom
willing to wither,

the dry creek bed, scrub forest,
hollows without their owls,

no quick, silent shadows
across the needle floor.

And when the brute who directs
all this said, *Work, blister, sweat,*

I acquiesced. Like I lacked
the right nutrient for being alive

or returned to some earlier form,
green and slippery,

that hadn't even slunk
from the water.

I hear the voice echo
through every plagued tree

but at last I know to call it vicious.
I dive off the rocks and swim deeper

until the pressure
beats inside my human skin.

When I rise and break the surface,
my lungs expand like wings.

Two

When Fog, When Mountain

So many cracks—
            my window is always open.
Heat and cold,
            electric saws, steeped ash leaves
and moths all drift in,
            but what's best is this:
the smell of a cloud.
            As if a mountain grew
beneath my bed
            while I dreamt of skyscrapers.

My train is now
            a country train, cradling coal
through mist.
            Here men masked in soot look
askance or long
            for me to bring them babies.
Here my mother
            endured five labors after me,
under moonshine
            kept on a high shelf.

This vapor world
            that knocks the glass—what has it
to do with me,
            a woman of the valley who
would rather
            the earth tower than kneel
before her?
            I would marry it, but the cloud smell
is a cruel smell:
            filling me with wanderlust, refusing
to touch my face.

Calling the Animal

What I can do cannot by me be done.
—Miguel de Guevara

The child thought she was alone.
Jackal slunk in, and the room went iron.
She felt him pin her legs and shoulders,
paws scratching her skin raw, breath
warm on her twitching face. Jackal said,
If you call me, nothing will be easy.
Leave me in the desert where I belong.
Leave me be, he said.

The Sound I'll Make

when I meet the devil will break the backs of bees. I'll say, Let the clatter come,
and it will be so. A dragged leg's rasp, a scrabbling rodent, a roiling kettle

of buzzards ready to gorge and preen. A bite through fruit skin, my sister's
window opened, the ocean in a lightning whelk flung across the morning.

Hound muzzle digging in fur, tongue at new wound, and down the avenue
sewers flood, churn, spill airplane bottles, dolls' heads, and dominoes.

Snap of linen on the line—sprung firmament. Spine against bleached
cement, rose rashes spreading, irresistible scratch. Suck of tar at ungulate foot,

the pavement split, a neighbor child in the sandbox belly, raking to the mantle.
Swing of scythes in lawn sculptures, gravel under gator heels, the clicking spin

of fan blades, slicing pruning shears, crackling toe joints and twigs, birled logs
down the pile, a mile of starlings muttering to themselves. But no sound

summoned will match the cat-gut strings, the singing claws, the horse's hair aflame.
Voice of my flesh crying up from the ground: a beat as soft as the beast himself.

Easter

Not the bloodied not the vultured
limbs standing three abreast
but a blanket on the grass

Daffodils and dyed blue eggs
children missed in flowerbeds
the fecal smell of fresh mulch

I stand and breathe the open air
craning towards the tree line
Everything is boundaries

and to be truly present
in my body is to be trapped inside
an execution chamber

The end of the body must be
the end full stop but I wish
the body were like an eggshell

Is belief something you can
fertilize
Is that the difference

between a yellow yolk for eating
and a feathered thing
swimming inside

Bath

When we had just a film of hair on our bodies
my sister and I would rub our bellies

together before jumping in the bubbled bath.
Stomachs round, chests flat—it was easy.

Our father would suds our hair into bunny ears
while I gave myself a hoary beard

and my sister perfected her foamy breasts.
Then we posed, listened to bubbles pop and vanish,

and laughed at the creatures we'd become
until Dad took the white pitcher from the basin,

poured warm water over our up-turned faces,
and changed us back into his girls.

Mary

A relative told me, *Place the Virgin in your kitchen window*
and no unwanted rain will come.

I found a plastic figurine in the junk shop and perched her
so she overlooked the gas station, fish shack, and laundromat.

The skies cleared on the day that mattered, the day my father
walked me to you while one hundred people watched.

We let him say a prayer that at times made us wince.
But still the weather put glory in our minds, glory in the breeze

and in the sun that shone but did not blaze
while we danced atop that pretty hill far from our home.

Mary looked across the parking lot's dingy cars
and sparkling litter, and I did not think of her.

If you don't take her from the window after, she'll bring
a hurricane or tornado—some kind of nasty weather.

When we returned as husband and wife
we couldn't help but move Mary to the table

full of small things we cherished, quick to collect dust.
We've had weeks of unremarkable weather since,

and if pressed, we would not announce that we believed.
But I would say the glory spared no corner of the city

while Mary stood on the sill—veiled, pliable, but undisturbed
in her blue dress, her celluloid arms outstretched.

El Río Manu

Just below the equator, night fell in minutes.
The sun dropped to the Manu's surface
then eased into the water, and the whir
of insects grew louder as shadows deepened.

Summer floods made an inverted forest
of the river: roots crawled starward,
branches reached for richer earth.
I was on the wrong side of Earth to be near you.

The sun burned where you were
and you must have sweat, while Venus glared
so close to me that it reflected on the water,
trailing light that led to shore. I shivered

as the blue-black Manu became our bedspread,
fallen trees flattened into our floors,
an eddy by a branch curved like your frown,
and my guide's shoulders turned into yours

as he stood at the stern and swung, from snag
to snag, the only artificial light for miles.
He slowed the boat, the motor now
a purr. I looked for jaguars.

Later, when we passed through
the last town for fuel, the only woman
on the beach without a baby in her arms
begged us to look for her son's body,

but we only saw caimans in the water, their eyes
shining red in the flashlight's beam.

Panther

When I say I won't
bring a life into this world,
my parents' faces
darken with disappointment.

Me on my father's shoulders,
in my mother's lap,
and the panther whispering,
One day you must carry them.

She Who Will Hurt Us

Call her black mold, millpond witch
Drainage ditch, the stench of decay

She's coming for our mother and father
Her fingers stretching towards their organs

What would happen if we loved her
If we clipped her fingernails

Washed her linens, wiped the spittle from her chin
She was never beautiful

Our hair glows in the evening sun
Our eyes widen with acuity

Through the keenness of your eyes
You will triumph and destroy

Her horse is black and riderless
Eating apples from our hands

A gale slaps our fresh faces, and soon
We are all dying again

Listen, mother and father
Take this horse and trample her very bones

A Warning

One summer day your neighbor went out with a gallon of ammonia
to destroy the wasp nest at the edge of his property.

He came to a granular mound of dirt in the grass
and poured the chemical down a finger-sized hole at the base.

The mound caved in
and then the ground—

the man did not know that mound was one of many openings
for a deep labyrinth of connected nests, and he had stood at the center.

He fell into their underworld. They covered his body
in a hooded, beaded robe and stung until he died.

This story overcomes me in moments of heart-stopping beauty,
when the bees are buzzing and the ground is alive,

when you are walking to the edge of our lawn in full sun.

Gravity

There will be no edges, but curves.
—Tracy K. Smith, "Sci-Fi"

In the beginning gases gathered

    into stars and galaxies spun

like hurricanes, collided, and grew until

    all I wanted was to lie

on the couch and read a book. That's how

    compulsory romantic love is:

all things with mass attract each other

    and even light gravitates.

My husband reaches for me at night,

    but it isn't he who holds me to earth.

Like every speck in the universe, I am bound

    in another's embrace.

Illiterate Dream

In the letter he says he wants me
to do something indecipherable.

Meanwhile I have to
play a cello, read the music,

use a futuristic hook-like bow
superfluous to my line of work.

In black and silver, players all around me
brush their strings with ease.

I can't read the music but I can hear it.

Cry for Help

with a line from Katerina Rudcenkova

Like a note written in the voice of the cat:
If you close this door, I can't get out!
That sort of thing.
Yes, I live inside the piano.

I used to hear screams from the street at night,
now I hear them midday. I look out,
see a group of people laughing.
My book describes moths
and mulberry trees.
I hush it.

How come *cry for help* is
she didn't mean to do it?
She did something, right?
Moths and mulberries piled around her,
filled up the tub.
If you close this door, I can't get out.

Landlocked

Men are building a prison in the east, between
window frames, between columns holding my home.

The sky is still a desert. I crave nights past
when jagged fingers played the firmament.

Last spring, the ceiling fell all around me.
I was sleeping then.

It rained inside a fortnight. My only life wrapped
in plastic, I careened through the house like a killer.

Trowel in one hand, drink in the other, I tended
houseplants with rotten roots, drowning in their pots.

Those days before I saved myself,
I divvied out longevity every time I drove nowhere.

Now the patched ceiling slopes like the roof
of a mine. Fissures, still visible, will not leak.

If I drowned, hypoxia would stop
the beating heart, quicker than you'd think.

When it is night in every crevice, camel crickets
rise like rats from a dry-docked ship.

The vermin's secret: not knowing
how dull it can be to thrive.

Against Me, with Me, Round About

Work

Inside the fowl, I feel for organs:
the hard gizzard, the soft heart.
My fingers seek the surface—
the hands know nothing here.

Body

Is it fair to brim over when given
a vessel? Inside—the soul; inside—
the lungs; inside—the brain.
How could they fit in a jar
on the mantel, even one
fashioned by a craftsman?

Home

Not a nest, a sycamore,
riparian, replanted nowhere
near a river. To prosper,
to bear fruit and family,
or molder at the trunk.
I must go to water.

Need

The red words, blue seas, in holy books.
Doubt like thunderstorms, like talons
in my shoulder. Keeping myself at great
remove, I found the monastic scribe's peace.
Through the window this morning:
a red-tailed hawk in the white tree
sat with me as the sun rose.
I had already taken up my instrument.

Something Like Belief

I call you with black doves, but no rain comes.
My voice is brittle as a bare tree against the sun.

When you sent the ark sailing over mountains,
the waters were heavens to the drowned below.

You may find me wicked yet.
You may find me any minute.

I see your face at night on the ceiling:
fluorescent halo left by a lamp extinguished.

The animal in my chest lopes through dry grasses.
It is neither fowl nor cattle nor creeping thing.

I wouldn't call it clean.
Even you regret, regretted our making.

Your shadow leaves a trench in the pavement,
and no one listens when I speak your name.

Listen. At last, the horses
gallop on the dappled roof.

My hand in yours—blue flame.
How easy to recoil.

I remain, and their hoof-falls fill my skull.
They are proof, or a cold front passing through.

A day gone, and a day coming, knocking.
Shall I let the vagrant in and feed him?

I have nothing to give. I give him the horses:
dripping manes, warm muzzles,

and the gallons of air in each lung.

Three

Real

I had no imaginary friends
Had large brown toads
Crayfish in the creek
Feet sinking in clay soil
Its sucking sounds
I loved what was real
The black snake that brushed
My skin as it fell
Rang in me a red alarm
You should know by now
I love the fear that fills my body
Would call it my friend
The slick cliffs my friend
Black widows in the woodpile
Rats I chased through culverts
The high pipe for sewage
Where I practiced balance
Fell on my back
In the briared ravine
I crossed the pipe again and again
Tiptoed through the air
I'm grown and gone
From that house in the woods
But dear danger
I know you're there

Coyote

Coyote creeping by the creek
Coyote I'm so tired
I would pray in the middle of a field
But not the middle of this room

Coyote in the thicket
Coyote in the closet
Coyotes just out of sight
Howl with ambulances

A carcass blocks the garden path
The velvet antlers of spring
Flies line the rigid ears
Coyote the house grows still

My bed exposed in the bare room
My body laid upon it
Coyote see the inside
The eyes behind the lids

Find in them desire
Find hunger
Yes I'm older I'm not finished
Coyote please come closer

Time passes but it does not move forward
—Marisa Silver, *Little Nothing*

The animals slide slowly around,
baring teeth in static snarls or grins.

My hair cut in thick, blunt bangs,
I bob in a mirror's glare

while organ music blares
from an invisible source.

I hate my horse, its clown colors
and relentlessness.

Guards stand at the circumference
so no child jumps off too soon.

The people I love wave from the lawn
as I am taken from them by degrees.

I am that girl and I am no longer.
Her knuckles are as white as mine

when I'm speeding on the beltway, caught
between a truck and a concrete barrier.

When the ride ends and I step off,
I feel earth spin beneath me still.

Marrow

At rest, his heart beats too fast. Heat envelops
our whole bed—a red splotch on an aerial map.

I want to look down on my sleeping self,
take her hand, and pull

until she stands before me.
To believe she is not sunk when the eyes go dark.

She will babble dream-speak like the creek I played in
as a child—black water blooming with garbage I loved.

A silver fork stuck in a sandbar is a treasure.
She will remember this fork.

She will know the future of the couple in bed—
the man with fire skin, the girl who aged and forgot.

Outside, an owl in the locust tree burrows deep inside itself
as if reaching for marrow.

Through all the nights I've slept while he lay awake,
has he come to know this woman I will never meet,

formed from scraps I've lost?
Memories, fears, and desires pile on her in layers

she strips away for him, not me, in his arms at night.
What does she tell him?

If I could hear her voice, I would never sleep again.

Onions

Is it possible to fall in love over a dish of onions?
—Graham Greene, *The End of the Affair*

I once knew a boy who would eat one like an apple—
a raw red onion that stained his lips purple.

You put them in each dish, because you know
exactly what I like.

The drama of the scent, the cry,
the warm, biting flavor and how it lingers.

This afternoon, we made love every which way
even though my back ached from making love the day before.

I fight the urge to smell my fingers on the train.
Every place smells of onions, every pore.

Marriage

For years I pronounced *timbre* like *timber.*
You pointed out the difference
weeks after our wedding

and I imagined the sound a maple makes
when it sings without strings stretched over its body.

It is not pitch, not volume,
but something deep inside the sound
that quivers.

My deepest fear:

that one day I won't be able to stand
the sight of you, the sound of your voice.

The maple chopped, stripped, sawed, and sanded.

You pick up the old guitar,
the one you got from a pawnshop before we met,
when we both were wild.

You play the same verse over and over,
changing a note each time, and it does get better.

Sitting in this cluttered room,
among objects that fill me with love
and revulsion for their familiarity,

the plain present strikes me like an ax.

There could have been so many versions of us,
why this one?

If we are to survive, we must be different people together,
a little different every day.

The ax in my side softens as you begin to sing.

Ice Mountain

Our next-door neighbors light a fire each night.
I use my nose as eyes and watch it burn.
Spring comes glacier slow, and the ants speak
in the substrate, woodpeckers in the willow oaks
bleating like zebras. It snows in the South now,
two good storms a winter, the city's one plow
like an aging thresher. I saw a boy climb Everest
in a parking lot—what a view that must have been.
There's the bike co-op, the condos under construction,
the tobacco barn turned farm-to-table restaurant.
Reaching the mountain's peak, the boy stepped back
as if surprised, slid down the pile of ice,
squealed in delight, and began to climb again.
He couldn't leave the asphalt fast enough.

Lightning-Struck Cypress

Each day on my run I stare where the cypress
grew colossal as a woolly mammoth.

It was struck down the trunk clean and straight—ruined
before that storm but I didn't know then—the bolt
drawn to moisture gathered at its rotting core.

I had thought it would outlive me, my favorite tree.
The current blasted off bark and branches.

When I ran the next morning I witnessed the killing:
men lopping off what was left. A wide scar shined
tusk-white as they brought the stripped trunk down.

Now a stump stands in the field, but behind waves
of summer heat I see the mammoth bristling. I feel
static electricity held in each hair of its coarse coat—
a conduit between what was and will be. The nothing.

An Ending

after Alice Notley's "The 'Feminine' Epic"

It is possible to stop

    the machine of destruction

        I kept telling myself this tale

The people I loved most

      began to speak inaudibly

        My mother's head

   turned like an owl's

      I felt the presence

   of untamed powers

        like a woman's voice

   with access to the dream

Finches slurred their calls

   My skin leapt up

      In dreams we chase

   the figment of a story

I boarded a train containing women   only women

   We were being given

      the desert

        its negative space

I want something greater than myself

a forest perhaps

or what's outside this globe

the system of threads

Or are they needles

Are they

a woman's hair

Each strand has an ending

Do we return there

Milkweed

I read your book on the hill where we met
as milkweed seeds rode drafts of air
sinking   lifting   gathering

In your eighties
your body growing
light again

your dearest friends dead or dying

I am getting on

In those pages
you wrote of childhood   old age

left out the middle

and the seeds sailed

Reading Wind

Two packages arrived at my door
in the hour evening fell.

It was a night of good fortune, the air
smooth and warm for winter, but soon

branches began to wave in gusts, dry leaves
cycloned, and my long hair blinded me.

I heard the words of a palm reader
who held my hand the night before:

Look within. And the wind blew
without me, but also within.

Mowing

The following is an erasure of Part Three, chapters II, IV, and V of Anna Karenina *by Leo Tolstoy, translated by Richard Pevear and Larissa Volokhonsky.*

II.

For him words took away the beauty of what he saw

    morning

        the horse's legs

                the enormous

   grey-green sea
            unstirred by wind

IV.

As he rode   the muzhiks came

              swinging their scythes

    sweat streamed down

his back
      soaked

    He thought of nothing

        another swath   another

              They lost

                    time

V.

        through the succulent grass

           The scythe cut by itself

               The old man

turned eastward to pray

            The sun   behind

              smelling of spice, the grass

in swaths

      his whole body

         a single blade

              that some external force moved

Aubade, Riparian

I went to the river for water
        as I had done in a former life
I still wanted you like I wanted the water
        the rush and music of this world

You were nowhere to be seen, but I could feel you running through—

If my body were a boat
        Look: my body is a boat
and you were the water
        Is the river at home on earth
                or is water a guest
                        always trying to leave?
I would not know how to turn back

Will

Sunset on stone
light in the pocket
one hand warming

the other
gloveless

lifts to the sky
without string
the hand remembers

how to offer
oneself to power

how to say
I'll go
I'll come away

     *

Waterfall curtain
over cave mouth

nearly a mirror

put your hand through
that other life

put your body through
and have it

The Woods Within

I.

Your home is a pine forest, given
to lightning fires, to needle blankets
and smoke skies. Seed cones drip pitch
down to fern spores while thin saplings
fight for sun. Blight has taken the ironwood
and beech, the storybook oaks.
In spring, candles shoot from your scales.

II.

To sleep here.
Or, to break from earth
if your roots are shallow.
Beneath the broad-bladed
grass: a worm song.
Those old beeches, their limbs
staggered like hart horns,
they were roped,
the oaks frilled with an ax.
Your bark ripples
as the winds gust.

III.

When the rope and the blade and the coming train,
when your grain is twisted, skin ugly, elephantine,
when you haven't the courage to hang to cut to jump
but instead lie without living, you ask if God,
as many times as you've been spared, has ever interfered.
Remember how you prayed as the tornado approached
and sidestepped your home. The brittle pine frames
of your windows, the billowing wood paneling
on your walls—how are you today, in the same room,
safe and warm? In time, this house will fall like timber
whether or not you're rooted to the bed.
Despite every weakness you've ever felt,
it is up to you to save yourself.

Thanks Be to Big Windows

Winter vegetables
on the windowsills

glass drawing lines
between warmth and cold

rottings and ripenings
drying leaves

our plain life pulled
out to the evening

branches ink-black in silhouette
the writing spider's finished web

inside and outside
the same if you squint

when I woke up in the morning
I knew exactly what I was

Notes

"Cyclops" was written after reading and is greatly indebted to Ocean Vuong's *Night Sky with Exit Wounds*, especially the poems "Immigrant Haibun," "Always & Forever," and "Homewrecker."

"Self-Portrait As a Beast with Two Backs" was inspired by Aristophanes's speech from Plato's *Symposium*, from *The Complete Works of Plato*, translated by Benjamin Jowett.

"The Ash Field" takes its epigraph from Jean Valentine's poem "To the Bardo" and was also inspired by her poem "Door in the Mountain."

"A Fine Essence Descending" owes its genesis to the following passage from *The Sufis* by Idries Shah, in which Shah explains the significance of imagery depicted on a coronation robe worn by Roger II, King of Sicily (1093–1154): "The palm tree (NaKHL) is chosen because the triconsonantal root NKHL also means 'a fine essence descending almost impalpably,' such as the divine element *baraka* or 'blessedness.' Words from the same root include sifted flour and a gentle drizzle of rain. Since the palm is a holy tree associated with birth among the Arabs, its appearance on a coronation robe means 'Source of Blessedness.'"

The title "*Disobedience / is the first right of being alive*" comes from Paisley Rekdal's poem "Why Some Girls Love Horses."

The epigraph of "Calling the Animal" is from Miguel de Guevara's poem "Raise me up, Lord," translated by Samuel Beckett.

Gratitude to Craig Popelars (who is not a relative, technically), whose advice inspired the poem "Mary."

In "Cry for Help," the line "*Yes, I live inside the piano*" is from Katerina Rudcenkova's poem "Yes, I live inside the piano," translated by Alexandra Büchler.

The fifth stanza of "Something Like Belief" was inspired by Genesis 6:20 (King James Version): "Of fowls after their kind, and of cattle after their kind, of every creeping thing of the earth after his kind, two of every sort shall come unto thee, to keep them alive."

In "An Ending," I have paraphrased or borrowed phrases from Alice Notley's "The 'Feminine' Epic," which was delivered as a talk at the New York State Writers Institute, SUNY Albany (October 1995).

"Aubade, Riparian" was written after reading *The Soul Is Here for Its Own Joy*, in which Robert Bly writes, "Often in the Sufi tradition, a distinction is made between the soul and the spirit. The soul is the intelligence that praises this world's beauty—its roses, its wine, its beautiful women and men, its poems and its prayers. The soul is a grateful guest of the earth. The spirit is imagined as a guest of the soul, who is constantly trying to leave."

"The Woods Within" is indebted to Alice Munro's story "Wood."

2007

Trick Pear, Suzanne Cleary
So I Will Till the Ground, Gregory Djanikian
Black Threads, Jeff Friedman
Drift and Pulse, Kathleen Halme
The Playhouse Near Dark, Elizabeth Holmes
On the Vanishing of Large Creatures, Susan Hutton
One Season Behind, Sarah Rosenblatt
Indeed I Was Pleased with the World, Mary Ruefle
The Situation, John Skoyles

2008

The Grace of Necessity, Samuel Green
After West, James Harms
Anticipate the Coming Reservoir, John Hoppenthaler
Convertible Night, Flurry of Stones, Dzvinia Orlowsky
Parable Hunter, Ricardo Pau-Llosa
The Book of Sleep, Eleanor Stanford

2009

Divine Margins, Peter Cooley
Cultural Studies, Kevin A. González
Dear Apocalypse, K. A. Hays
Warhol-o-rama, Peter Oresick
Cave of the Yellow Volkswagen, Maureen Seaton
Group Portrait from Hell, David Schloss
Birdwatching in Wartime, Jeffrey Thomson

2010

The Diminishing House, Nicky Beer
A World Remembered, T. Alan Broughton
Say Sand, Daniel Coudriet
Knock Knock, Heather Hartley
In the Land We Imagined Ourselves, Jonathan Johnson
Selected Early Poems: 1958-1983, Greg Kuzma
The Other Life: Selected Poems, Herbert Scott
Admission, Jerry Williams

2011

Having a Little Talk with Capital P Poetry, Jim Daniels
Oz, Nancy Eimers

Working in Flour, Jeff Friedman
Scorpio Rising: Selected Poems, Richard Katrovas
The Politics, Benjamin Paloff
Copperhead, Rachel Richardson

2012
Now Make an Altar, Amy Beeder
Still Some Cake, James Cummins
Comet Scar, James Harms
Early Creatures, Native Gods, K. A. Hays
That Was Oasis, Michael McFee
Blue Rust, Joseph Millar
Spitshine, Anne Marie Rooney
Civil Twilight, Margot Schilpp

2013
Oregon, Henry Carlile
Selvage, Donna Johnson
At the Autopsy of Vaslav Nijinksy, Bridget Lowe
Silvertone, Dzvinia Orlowsky
Fibonacci Batman: New & Selected Poems (1991-2011), Maureen Seaton
When We Were Cherished, Eve Shelnutt
The Fortunate Era, Arthur Smith
Birds of the Air, David Yezzi

2014
Night Bus to the Afterlife, Peter Cooley
Alexandria, Jasmine Bailey
Dear Gravity, Gregory Djanikian
Pretenders, Jeff Friedman
How I Went Red, Maggie Glover
All That Might Be Done, Samuel Green
Man, Ricardo Pau-Llosa
The Wingless, Cecilia Llompart

2015
The Octopus Game, Nicky Beer
The Voices, Michael Dennis Browne
Domestic Garden, John Hoppenthaler
We Mammals in Hospitable Times, Jynne Dilling Martin
And His Orchestra, Benjamin Paloff

Know Thyself, Joyce Peseroff
cadabra, Dan Rosenberg
The Long Haul, Vern Rutsala
Bartram's Garden, Eleanor Stanford

2016
Something Sinister, Hayan Charara
The Spokes of Venus, Rebecca Morgan Frank
Adult Swim, Heather Hartley
Swastika into Lotus, Richard Katrovas
The Nomenclature of Small Things, Lynn Pedersen
Hundred-Year Wave, Rachel Richardson
Where Are We in This Story, Sarah Rosenblatt
Inside Job, John Skoyles
Suddenly It's Evening: Selected Poems, John Skoyles

2017
Disappeared, Jasmine V. Bailey
Custody of the Eyes, Kimberly Burwick
Dream of the Gone-From City, Barbara Edelman
Sometimes We're All Living in a Foreign Country, Rebecca Morgan Frank
Rowing with Wings, James Harms
Windthrow, K. A. Hays
We Were Once Here, Michael McFee
Kingdom, Joseph Millar
The Histories, Jason Whitmarsh

2018
World Without Finishing, Peter Cooley
The End of Spectacle, Virginia Konchan
Big Windows, Lauren Moseley
Immortal Village, Kathryn Rhett
Last City, Brian Sneeden
Black Sea, David Yezzi